30 Days
of
Real

David Carruthers

Extreme Overflow Publishing
Dacula, GA
USA

Extreme Overflow
PUBLISHING
Dacula, GA
USA

Extreme Overflow Publishing
A Brand of Extreme Overflow Enterprises, Inc
P.O. Box 1811
Dacula, GA 30019

www.extremeoverflow.com
Send feedback to info@extreme-overflow-enterprises.com

Printed in the United States of America

Editors: Michele Saunders & Paige Smith
Photo by Jerome King/Imprint Boston
Cover Design by Charles Seagraves/Imprint Boston

Library of Congress Catalogin-Publication
Data is available for this title. ISBN: 978-0-692-13867-0

This book is dedicated to

Todd Wigfall and Jerome King for keeping it

real with me which has produced great friendships.

Foreword

This book-devotional that David writes is a very practical application for everyday living. Not promising us the moon but assuring the reality of what good habits can develop in us to make positive influence and become all that God has called us to be.

Every quote challenges us to look inward and then invites you to begin to think differently. So we will mature and grow in those weak struggling areas we don't share or want to face.

If you as a reader, apply these principles and take these challenges seriously, you will have intentional change. You will see a great difference and a shifting in your focus. Your mindset and even your imagination of your dreams will be a reality. David, thank you for challenging us and even stretching us in areas we were in denial of and afraid to confront within ourselves.

Wayne L. Shirk, Senior Pastor
New Hope Assembly

I love this book! I love it so much that I will read it again, one day at a time. It's honest, funny, sad and uplifting, just like life is. It reminds us of what is important to stay focused on through whatever life throws at us, bad or good. And that paying attention is not only recommended, but required. Thank you for the great read!

Elise Pashigian, International Business Woman, Owner of Massage Envy

~~~~~~~

The news stories and images all around us today make facing reality a frightening, dismal prospect. David Carruthers changes all this in 30 Days Of Real. In a spiritual and practical guidebook, David shows us how to maximize our value from the inside out and offers us an invitation to embark on a life-changing journey filled with possibilities. Presented in bite-size portions over 30 days, this book makes it easy for readers to distill the potent nuggets into daily contemplation and practice.

Through the wit and wisdom of David's own experience, we are challenged to enter into the real stuff of life with spiritual vision and positive action. The inescapable message of this book is that we can engage and transform our ordinary struggle into extraordinary greatness. Thankfully, amidst the corruption of vision and co-opting of hope in our world today, David has provided for us a valuable and timeless resource from a wide variety of faith traditions and religious backgrounds will return to these writings over and over again when seeking to energize their lives with renewed purpose.

Kathleen S. Verna, Senior Pastor
PureSpring Global Commission
President & Co-Founder,
CrossTown Church International

~~~~~~~

This book is brilliant! Valuable lessons to women! I love the way you skillfully break down the alphabet. One thing that stood out to me is "Live Your Dreams." Someone reading this will be challenged to be less fearful and to be who they were born to be.

Real nuggets in "Broken Beauty." I like "SLOW DOWN" and your readers will. We make ourselves busier than we should be and we miss out on what is really important. Lots of people need to hear this; we are a country that stays on the treadmill of life.

Thank you for the definition of "Greatness." The entry on "Kryptonite" is important. Knowing who I am, helps to understand who I am not. One of my favorite parts of this book is "Understanding Your Value." 30 Days Of Real has great insight.

Edriss Webbe, Senior Pastor
Ebenezer House of Worship

"30 Days Of Real" is more than a devotional. It's a roadmap of long lasting change. It's a unique read because it also goes the extra mile and provides practical suggestions everyone can use.

Troy Goode, Executive Pastor,
Destiny Christian Fellowship

Acknowledgement

I love God because His love for me is insane!

To my mother Cynthia Carruthers - A Rock!

My daughters,
Paige Smith & Leilah Carruthers, (Smuckoms).

Todd Wigfall, Jerome King,
Bishop John M. Borders III, Thomas I. Hinds,
Steve & Cheryl Galloway, Barbara Barrow Murray,
Darren Lucas, Derek Marshall, Elise Pashigian,
Pamela Gillard and Karen Lurie.

To the haters, thank you so much;
you have no idea how much you inspire me.

The "Real" ABC's

A is Always. Always strive to be your best from the inside out. This improves your character.

B is Believe. Believe in yourself and greatness will come to you.

C is Count. Count your blessings. Don't be like most people and take everyday things and people for granted.

D is Don't. Don't listen to the haters and doubters who do not believe in you. This will prove to be detrimental later.

E is Excellence. Strive for Excellence. Les Brown said, "If you reach for the stars, you'll land on the moon."

F is Fear. Run toward your fears and you will conquer them. If you run from your fears, you will fail.

G is Go. This word speaks of action. Always go toward your dreams.

H is Happiness. Happiness is contingent on things. Joy comes from within.

I is Institute. Institute rules, laws and principles in your life over feelings and opinions.

J is Jesus. He is Everything you need!

K is Keep. Keep love; kindness; justice; faithfulness and laughter near you.

L is Love. The best description of Love is in 1 Corinthians 13. Read it.

M is Monopoly. Play an older version of this game. It will teach you and your children about money. The more modern versions have credit cards. Stay away!

N is No. A powerful word that should be used frequently for people who take you away from your dreams and goals.

O is Omit. Omit: fear, jealousy, hatred, envy, and relational competing out of your life. They are dream killers.

P is Personal. Remember everything that you do is personal.

Q is Quiet. Respect the need for quiet time.
A Chinese proverb once said, "Think twice and say nothing."

R is Respect. Respect is given. Honor is earned.

S is Slowly. Your dreams come to pass slowly. So, respect the process.

T is Tumultuous. This word means "uproar, full of ups and downs." Life is guaranteed to bring you this.

U is Unity. How powerful we all would be if we would unite.

V is Violence. Those who live by this sword, will die by it.

Y is Youth. Don't waste it. It is here today and gone tomorrow.

Z is Ziplock. It is a word worth twenty-four points in Scrabble and a good bag for the kitchen.

Now you know your ABCs, next time won't you sing with me.

Introduction

"Do your own thing on your own terms
and get what you came here for."

- Oliver James

Okay, as Steve Harvey would say, "Straight talk, no chaser." Welcome to the version we amicably call You. That can either scare the crap out of you depending on the voices you've been listening to or it can thrill you to elation.

Here's the great news! It only takes twenty-one days to a form a new habit[1], many of which you already have. So, think about that for a minute. Twenty-one days toward new and better financial decisions. Twenty-one days to better communication with the ones you love. Twenty-one days for a better sex life-yeah, multiple smiley faces. Twenty-one days towards a new body. Twenty-one days to the you who is deep

---

[1]   Guitierrrez, Jason, "Pick the Brain, Grow Yourself," www.pickthebrain.com/blog/how-long-it-really-takes-to-form-a-new-habit-and-how-to-get-started

down waiting to surge and stay at the surface.

So, Dave, why did you choose the number thirty? Because there are thirty days in a month and quite frankly, that was the original idea. Thirty days to not only form a habit but potentially begin to create a new lifestyle; a new perspective; and reconnect with not a new, but an authentic You!

Now let me say this. I am not promising you or stating at the least that in one month your life will be amazing. No! Please understand that there are no shortcuts to success on any level in life.

What I am promising you, however, is that once you develop the habit of examining your actions, you will realize that as you have begun to diligently work on those small decisions that later become giants that are now impeding your destiny. You will find that over a short period of time you will slowly improve.

Some of these habits include negative thinking and talking; arguing over petty things; not cleaning up after yourself; not exercising even though you have the gym membership; talking back; not following through and I'm sure the list could go on.

The Reverend Dwight L. Moody once stated, "I

have had more trouble with myself than with any other man." However, it is vital to give yourself credit for little improvements because there are no big achievements without the little steps. For instance, I never thought I could be an author and yet you are reading one of my four, published books. Every book that was ever written by any author was done so one word, one page at a time.

Likewise, I never thought I could be a television host and yet I hosted one program for over seven years. If it happened for me, then your dreams can definitely happen for you. There is greatness in you!

Treat 30 Days Of Real as a thirty-day devotional that you can use all year round. Us it as a tool to include in your book club to ask questions and gain a deeper understanding on the many challenges of life. Use it as a guide for going to the next level. Share it with your friends; enemies; coworkers; and spouses.

The beauty in you having this book and applying it is simple: The You who waits to emerge is incredible. You will be shocked but thoroughly pleased once you get real with yourself. You will not want to retreat to what you used to be. You will be amazed at what growth can do.

You will attract people you never thought you could and people will do things for you because you inspire them. That is a glimpse of what is in store for you. You have the potential for "amazing." In the words of John Mason, "You were born an original. Don't die a copy."

Contents

Cont'd

Welcome to
30 Days Of Real!

Day #1

Day #1
Live Your Dreams!

—————————————

.⌒■⌒.

"Go confidently in the direction of
your dreams! Live the life you've imagined."

– *Henry David Thoreau*

I was at a conference in Atlanta years ago where I saw the great Bishop T.D. Jakes speak. At a particular monumental moment he was praying over Marvin Sapp and at the end of the prayer he said, "Live Your Dreams!" I said to myself, "That's impossible."

As soon as I said it, I heard a voice say, "Is that because of the way you think?" I wrestled with those words and found myself in a trance. Even when he continued speaking, I couldn't get my mind off that phrase: Live Your Dreams. The prayer Bishop Jakes spoke was filled with such powerful words. I never heard someone say something that bold with such confidence.

After the seminar was over, I went to my hotel room and still couldn't get that saying off my mind. I was stricken. I said to myself, "No one speaks like that" and I'm definitely not going to hear people talk like that when I get back to Boston. I decided that I couldn't let the phrase die in Atlanta. I began saying it to myself. I put it on my answering machine and the next thing I knew, "Live Your Dreams" became my mantra.

It's a big statement, but I realized that the more I studied it and listened to people say it, that there are always aspects of our dreams that we are living right now. This is so very important to realize. Great people talk bigger, think better and therefore live bigger.

They are not better than us. However, they actually believe what they say. Sammy Davis Jr. said, "Either you are committed to your dreams or your fears." Jimmy Kimmel stated that his ex-wife asked him concerning his dreams, "What is the Plan B?" He said to her, "There is no Plan B. There is only Plan A."

When you have that attitude, you live your dreams. Most people are not serious about what they really want or need. They let life get in the way. I call them giants. It is why others say things like, "Excuses are the tools of the incompetent and they that use them rarely excel in anything but excuses."

Your dreams are hard work but they aren't what is worth pursuing. The sweet victory of maintaining your vision despite the obstacles is what makes the dream so marvelous. Also, it is the pursuit that builds your character. This is the most important factor that many fail to realize.

This is not the lottery. You can't just sporadically "play" and hope to win. It takes determination, sweat, money, failure and persistence. Commitment to this process is what separates the great from the mediocre.

Writing books now for me is easy and fun. However, my first book, "Kill Your Giants," took me five years to write, during which time I told God several times that He "had the wrong person." Obviously, He was right and I was wrong.

You should put yourself around people who

believe in you and in your dreams. Your emotional environment needs good soil for your dreams to flourish. My mother always would take me with her a lot of places as a teenager. However, she would always respect when I said I was writing because she would let me be.

You need people to respect who you are and see it. In the book, "The One Thing," Gary Keller talks about blocking out time, say four hours, for example, so that you can do what you do best every day for at least five days a week. It is what some of the greatest entertainers and writers do. So, I emulated it.

So, the question is, what are you really good at?

What is the one thing that you would do whether you got paid or not?

What are you passionate about?

There is no better time than now to take action toward your goals and dreams. Write them down! Take the journey seriously, but have fun doing it. Always recognize that there are aspects to your dreams that you have that you are experiencing now, like good health; friends and family who support you; a job; opportunities that will and can make you better.

Being grateful also is huge to success. When you do these things, it will lighten the load when things get hard. But continue going after your dreams and build them one day at a time. Your joy will increase because you'll realize that you are closer to obtaining them. As Josie Spinardi said, "Create the life you can't wait to wake up to." This starts now beloved. Don't wait a moment longer. Live Your Dreams!

Scripture Meditation:

*"Now unto Him who is able to do exceeding abundantly above all we can ask or think,
according to the power that works within us,"*

Ephesians 3:20 (KJV)

Day #2

Day #2

Find Your Place

"Sometimes when you lose your way,
you find YOURSELF."

– Mandy Hale

I love this quote because it speaks a powerful truth. Life's tumultuous challenges are not designed to make us bitter, but better. And if they don't, that means you are not paying attention and you are out place.

Everyone goes through pain. However, great people allow the pain to propel them to their purpose. This is what all of the superhero movies have in common. Without the pain factor, they would just be regular people.

According to Worldometer[2], there are over seven billion people on this planet. Yet, according to authors Paul D. Tieger, Barbara Barron and Kelley Tieger in 16Personalities[3], there are only sixteen different personality types. Finding your personality type is essential, not only to your career and ministry, but according to various books written on psychology, and necessary in order to enhance and sharpen who you are.

Many of us hear powerful information on different subjects which is great. The problem is, however, we forget what we've heard within hours because of our busy lifestyles. Due to the fact that we have so much information coming at us, we have to think about what we're thinking about.

One has to be selective if they are going to be powerful. There are several ways to do this:

- **When you hear something powerful, write it down.** This will enhance our minds so that we don't forget.

---

[2] http://www.worldometers.info/world-population/?
[3] https://www.16personalities.com/

- **Watch great shows over and over again.** You never get it the first time. Repetitive action is the mother of skill.

- **Hang out with good people.** Birds of a feather flock together. You cannot expect great things to come from you if you're hanging around with losers and toxic people.

- **Read good books continually.** Readers are leaders. Most great people read at least one book a month.

- **Exercise.** It's great for our health and our minds.

- **Listen to your pain.** Pain is a wonderful teacher. It explains why we do what we do and what we should and should not do.

The best way to find your place in life is to discover what you are most passionate about and why. Also, the things that get you angry and you feel you should either stand up for, or reject with fervor are indications of where you are supposed to be.

Knowing this will set a spark in your life and put you on a journey toward continual bliss. Dancers dance. Singers sing. Writers write. What is your form of expression to the world?

Once you know and answer this, peace is inevitable. So is greatness. You will finally know the value that you bring and your place to bring it.

Day #3

_____

Day #3
Foundations

"I believe that home and marriage is the foundation of
our society and must be protected."
– Billy Graham

"Fear is the foundation of safety."
– Tertullian

What's your M.O.? Your modus operandi (M.O.) is
your mode of operation. Everybody has one. It causes
you to do what you do.

A challenge though is that your M.O. is subliminal.
We don't speak about it much, but it's not like a mantra.

Your mode of operation is your belief system; how you value things; how you will conduct your life, and what you will build your relationships on. If it is not intentional, then it will vary from situation to situation. This is very dangerous.

Years ago you would hear people say things like, "I'm Jamaican," or "We're Italians," or "We're Christians, we don't believe in that." Statements like these defined you. They said that you had some sort of foundation and there were things that you did or did not do.

Today is another story. People base their foundations on their feelings. Joyce Meyer stated, "Your emotions are very unstable and should never be the foundation of your life." A powerful truth! Leading our lives with our emotions has led to statistics like: more people being single now more than ever before in history; more Black men in jail than we have in college; and suicide being the third-leading cause of death among young people.

Marriage used to be the bedrock of this country. It was an institution where children felt safe and whole. Now we have swingers and young people who are not getting married and gender identity being taught in kindergarten.

If this is what America calls going forward, this is horrific and pathetic. We have reality shows that display to our young people that giving full vent to their anger is cool and not knowing how to reason is okay. Proverbs 29:1 (NIV) states, "A fool gives full vent to his anger." However, this display is glorified on TV and society goes where the media goes.

Proverbs was written by King Solomon. God told him, "No one will ever surpass your wisdom or riches." Now, comparing the media to Proverbs is like comparing apples to oranges. The media has a lot of people who don't represent Christ even though America was founded on Christian principles. Thomas Jefferson stated, "No nation has ever yet existed or been governed without religion. Nor can it be. The Christian religion is the best religion that has ever been given to man, and I as Chief Magistrate of this nation am bound to give it the sanction of my example." Well said Mr. President.

What is your foundation?

_____

_____

_____

_____

_____

Are the people in your life dependable and good examples for you to follow?

_____

_____

_____

_____

_____

Day #4

Day #4
Broken Beauty

.⌐ ■ ⌐.

"But he who dares not to grasp the thorn should never crave the rose."

- Anne Brontë

One of Tupac Shakur's famous poems was entitled, "The Rose That Grew From Concrete." It speaks of how one has surmounted great opposition and still achieved greatness even though it seemed impossible. We are surrounded by a plethora of testimonies and stories of how people have beaten the odds.

Christians have heard and recounted the amazing

stories of our forefathers, including Abraham, who waited one hundred years for a son and never wavered in faith. Job lost everything he had and was severely attacked in his physical body but didn't curse God. Stephen was stoned to death and said in his last breath in Acts 7:60, "Lord, do not hold this sin against them."

We cheer people at games. We pay people to see; to hear; to sing and act their stories. We clearly see over and over, and know that before we reach smooth sailing, there will be stormy seas. Yet when it comes to allowing God to build our stories, we complain and retreat back to mediocrity.

So I have come to give you a friendly reminder that gold is refined through fire. There is a dying process that one must undergo in order to receive life. There are no shortcuts to success. Great finances; great sex; great relationships or whatever you want to become great at must be built over time.

Today nobody wants to put in their dues. People look at great marriages for example, and say to themselves "I want that," without seeing the many disappointments and concessions behind closed doors. By the time anything is presented in public, there are many rehearsals. It is the performer's way of saying, "You will pay me for what you are too lazy to do."

The quote above is an important one because it speaks of counting the cost. Before the New England Patriots were a dynasty, they had one of the worst records of the National Football League. Babe Ruth struck out more than anyone in history. He also scored the most home runs than anyone in history. But the gem is that he never would have been the greatest, if at first, he wasn't the worse. This is why we should not despise humble beginnings. They are our learning springboards.

So in this game called life where pain is inevitable, perspective will be paramount. Life will bring us to a point where we will be broken. That point will not be the time to remain angry, but a time to reflect and ask God for wisdom. It is not what you go through; it is how we go through that determines your victory and whether you pass the test to go the next level.

If you complain during the storm, you may have to take the test over again. So pursue those who are wise, patient, and joyful because these are your guides. Accept brokenness as a bridge. Once you begin to do this you will see yourself in the beautiful light that you have been created to shine in and you will sail on the shores of mastery so that you can teach others.

I see you in the future, and you look beautiful.

Day #5

Day #5
Are You Too Busy?

.⌒■⌒.

"The new disease of our age is
being OK doing everything at the same time."
– Nigel Cumberland

With today's technology, texting and social media have become the new communication. We've become so impersonal with our gadgets that we don't recognize when we are being rude. It is common to go into a lunchroom with several people and everyone is on their phones.

A woman texted me at 4 PM and asked whether I wanted to go out that same evening, to which I replied, "Yes." After conversation only via text she responded that dinner or drinks were not going to work. We then decided on a movie at 10 PM. She stated that she would be free by 7:30. I said I would pick her up at 8:45 to which she replied, "I'll be on the go."

I said, "We should do this another time," to which she said, "I just need to make a stop and show my face." I asked where this place was. She said the address of the movie to which I replied again, "We should do this another time." She responded by saying, "That's why I hate texting," but I was following her lead.

She said she would call in a minute and then said by text that she can't call. That left me wondering what was really going on. It sounds like Craig D. Lounsbrough was right when he said, "Most of our fears are borrowed. Since that's the case we should get busy returning them."

What's probably more interesting is that I had a client for a massage earlier that day. I told her that I was supposed to go on a date that night and I wouldn't be surprised if it didn't happen. It didn't. And this was not the first time.

People use texting to not say or face what is really

going on. It allows you to escape confrontation. Oil Anderson states, "There are two kinds of busy:

1. Constantly distracting yourself from what is true;

2. Constantly working to create something real."

Are you so busy that you're running from yourself?

Are there no good men out there, or do the real ones intimidate you?

Is your busyness an indication that there is something you need to deal with but won't?

Alan Cohen states, "No one is too busy to do what they actually prefer." Why is that quote important? Plainly put, because many are missing out on great people and great moments because we are not focused on that which matters.

There are more singles today than ever before in history. A main reason for that is because a lot of people took other people for granted. At my mentor's funeral, I saw men weeping because they never took the time to appreciate a great man who poured into them. Now that he's gone, they will unfortunately never have the chance.

SLOW DOWN.

Don't let the media and life take your focus off loving and appreciating people. Busy doesn't mean more productive, it just means busy. Being busy causes you to be on overload and you miss out. The more you slow down, the more you appreciate life and its precious moments. An old man told me, "David, live your life; because eighty will get here like this." I believe him because age forty got here "like this."

Day #6

Day #6
What Is Greatness?

"Those who know their God shall do great exploits."
– Daniel 11:32

This is probably one of the most unasked questions by people but it yields massive importance. When we think of greatness, our minds automatically go to the ones who are rich and famous and those that have achieved extraordinary bounds. But greatness doesn't stop there because if it did, then ninety percent of the world would be excluded.

The word great is defined as, "superior; excellent; grand; beyond the average or uncommon." When we think of those words, our heavenly Father easily comes to mind, but here's the great news: we are created in His image. The fact of the matter is, we all have greatness in us. There are great things that we do daily but we just don't realize it. This is a vital mistake.

To not be cognizant of one's greatness is to not recognize your own worth. For the single mother who cooks for her children three times a week; picks them up from school; reads one child a bedtime story; helps another with their homework and coaches her daughter about boys, is that not greatness? To the man who works forty to sixty hours a week; comes home every day to his wife; ignores the other ladies who cross his path; guides and loves his children with fatherly wisdom and is a faithful member of his church, is that not greatness?

The problem with many of us is that we are looking for some major event to be able to state, "Oh, that was great," when greatness is staring us right in our faces. We quickly complain about a problem but rarely praise the things that are consistently good. This is a sure and unquestionable way to push great things and people away from us.

Jesus said in Mark 6:4, "A prophet is without honor

only in his hometown." Why? Because those who are closest to us take us for granted.

Remember, it was the haters who said of Jesus, "Oh, isn't this the brother of James? Isn't this the carpenter's son? What good can come out of Nazareth?" (Matthew 13:55-57)

Despite the haters and naysayers, you must never forget that there is greatness in you! You must say that out loud until you believe it and then ask the Holy Spirit to show you where it is.

He will probably show you things you've already been doing. Don't despise it. From my ability to write songs and poems, I wrote two books. I then became a speaker and then a TV host and producer. Those are amazing accomplishments that I never planned. God will increase you if you are faithful with what He has already given you.

In order for you to see your greatness, you must remove negative people from your environment. If you don't, your focus will always be on trying to prove yourself to them or they will simply drain your positive, creative energy.

So, there you have it. The next time you think of

greatness, think of yourself and if someone asks you, "What is greatness?" Simply reply, "That's me."

Write down four things that are great about you:

1. _____
   _____
   _____

2. _____
   _____
   _____

3. _____
   _____
   _____

4. _____
   _____
   _____

Day #7

Day #7

What's Your Kryptonite?

It is very unwise for you not to know your weaknesses. It is a very expensive ignorance that will cost you spiritually, financially, and relationally. I've seen marriages collapse; young men go to youth prison and then get incarcerated again, and I've seen people lose houses and commit suicide because they did not recognize and understand their flaws.

You cannot ignore your Kryptonite, it is just too costly. Kryptonite was a fictional chemical substance detailed in comic books that caused the superhero

Superman to lose his strength and to become weak. The word "Kryptonite" is also used as a slang term that refers to whatever makes a person weak. Superman did not ignore his Kryptonite. So, what makes you so special?

The purpose of understanding your weaknesses is not to magnify your pain but to protect your power. Every coach knows this. They understand that their sole responsibility is to highlight their players' greatness; minimize their players' weaknesses; and expose the weaknesses of their opponents. Whoever does this best wins the game. For example, the goal in beating the New England Patriots is to penetrate their offensive line and get to Tom Brady. If a team can't do that, they're going to lose.

There is a power in knowing who you are. For example, knowing that you are always on time; or a great cook; or always smiling. However, knowing who you are also means knowing who you are not. One must have the confidence to be able to say, "That is not my gift," or "I need help in . . ., etc." When you do this, you empower others because you are acknowledging their gift to fulfill your need and to strengthen your cause.

You can't do it all. It is foolish to think otherwise. Everyone has a team, whether they know it or not. If you're married, your spouse is a part of your team. If you have a best friend, they are a part of your team.

The importance of having a team is that it covers your Kryptonite. Everyone has weaknesses, but some are more exposed than others because they didn't value those around them. Brother Yun said it perfectly, "It is not great men who change the world, but weak men in the hands of a great God."

A poor perspective can be a huge Kryptonite. Humility is not weakness. It is a great power that will lead to inevitable greatness. It is very sad today to see so many being so quick to be rude, vulgar and hateful, thinking that it's powerful, when such behavior actually displays foolishness. Tragically, the media only further attributes to this prideful culture of folly. As TenTen ©, a Naruto character created by Masashi Kishimoto said, "The weaker you are, the louder you bark."

Maybe unforgiveness is your Kryptonite. Mahatma Gandhi once stated, "The weak can never forgive. Forgiveness is the attribute of the strong." Remember

Kryptonite has the potential to kill Superman. Forgiveness is greatness because it sets you free. You don't want your Kryptonite to kill you because you never acknowledge it and in doing so leave your soul unprotected. That would make you a dead man or woman walking.

What's your Kryptonite? For example:

_____

_____

_____

_____

_____

Scripture Meditation:

> *"Search me, God, and know my heart;*
> *test me and know my anxious thoughts.*
> *See if there is any offensive way in me,*
> *and lead me in the way everlasting."*
>
> *Psalms 139: 23-24*

Reflections:

Day #8

Day #8

Turn Pain Into Profit

"Losers quit when they're tired.
Winners quit when they've won."

– Mike Ditka

Pain in life is inevitable. What is yet to be determined is how you will deal with it. This is what truly separates the men from the boys and the women from the girls.

Anyone can give up when it's tough. Unfortunately, we have too many people who do that. This is why they get mediocre results in life. My personal definition of success is doing the opposite of what most people do. Most people self-sabotage when they're in pain. One of the ways they do this is by listening to people who don't empower them. They don't get the right counseling. Therefore the problem stays or transfers to the next relationship.

Problems don't go anywhere until you deal with them. You can't drink them away; sex them away; fight them away; or talk them away. You have to process them; discover the problem's sources and take the necessary measures to get healed. The process seems long but the benefits will last a lifetime.

Most people don't think long-term which is why the pain never leaves. They might settle for things to bring temporary pleasure or relief instead of allowing time and the process to heal them which can take them from good to great.

You must turn pain into profit. It is what winners do. Understand the perspective of pain. Charlie Chaplin said, "To truly laugh, you must be able to take your pain and play with it!" This is greatness because it doesn't state that the pain will leave. There is some pain in our lives that we have to live with and manage. Loved ones who pass away; divorce; growing up in toxic environments; being abused - the list can go on. Much of these we have no control over but how we respond to them is our choice. It is also paramount to our future. We are the summation of our choices. The quality of our lives depends on them.

Turning pain into profit means ensuring that you bounce back in a healthy way from what you have gone through. This is what some of our classic songs, such as, "I'm a Survivor," "I'll Get Over You," or "Killing Me Softly" are all about. Many relationships and marriages fail because people have soul ties or simply haven't gotten over the previous mate. As a result today, we have more singles than ever before in history. That's pain not profit.

As we get older, we must realize the value of good marriages and the importance of family. Unfortunately, in this society we only think of profit as money. A terrible mistake! Arthur Miller observed, "Don't be seduced into thinking that that which does not make a profit is without value." Value is all around us and in us if you are paying attention. This book can be one of many that sit on people's shelves and they never get around to reading it or it can be a life changer. The difference between poverty, mediocrity and greatness is determined by the value that one receives and applies. With that, I leave you with the words of Harper Lee, "Many receive advice, only the wise profit from it."

Quotes of the Day:

"The successful man will profit from his mistakes and try again in a different way."

– Dale Carnegie

"Wisdom has built her house; she has set up her seven pillars."

Proverbs 9:1

Reflections:

_____

_____

_____

_____

_____

_____

_____

_____

_____

_____

_____

Day #8

_____

_____

_____

_____

_____

Day #9

Day #9
You Have Sixty Seconds!

"Be who you are, everyone else is already taken."
- Oscar Wilde

"Make the most of yourself . . . for that is all there is of you."
– Ralph Waldo Emerson

In business they have this script called the "elevator pitch." It is called such because a lot of key men were extremely busy and you would only have time to tell them your business idea in the elevator. These rides would take no longer than thirty seconds.

It was in this amount of time that you could rise or fall depending on the power and savvy of your pitch. This was monumental because it could take you to the next level. I'm a super nice guy so I'm going to give you three options to tell me who you are in sixty seconds. You have thirty seconds to tell me your dreams, goals, and passions. Tell me your talents, your gifts. In these thirty seconds you can dream as big as you possibly want because after all, they are your dreams and if you don't think big of them, who will?

Let me also give you a couple of pointers. I would suggest that you write them down. Put your dreams on the wall with attractive pictures. Now, remember this: it is a pitch, therefore, rehearse this over and over again. That way you have your speech down to a science in thirty seconds or less.

Next, you have twenty seconds to tell me why you are doing this. What qualifies you for this dream? This job? It has been said that the "why" is the driving motivation behind your "do." This is where your passion seat is. Your "why" is your fuel. It is your deep sense of belief. It is the thing that drives your life.

Coretta Scott King was asked if she would marry again. She emphatically replied, "It was my mission to be married to Dr. Martin Luther King Jr." There are too many people who don't have a why in life. This causes them to live low lives. Please don't be one of them. Life is guaranteed to bring you pain but how you respond to it is key. Maya Angelou said, "You may not control all the events that happen to you, but you can decide not to be reduced by them." Let the "whys" of life always drive you back to your purpose. The more you rehearse this, the more powerful your twenty seconds will be.

Finally, you have ten seconds to tell me who you are not. Every great leader knows his or her flaws or shortcomings. No one person can play every position. He or she must have others around them to fill in the gaps where they fall short. In doing this, it will keep you humble and cognizant of the need to have others help you. It will also keep you focused on what you're great at so you can employ others to do what you're not so good at doing. Your sixty seconds is up.

Day #10

Day #10

This Process Called Forgiveness

*"All villains have this one thing in common;
they don't forgive."*

I have seen a lot of great movies in my life that depict the dichotomy between good and evil. What I have noticed is that all villains have this one thing in common: they do not forgive. There was an event in their lives that caused them massive hurt and pain. However, they were not able to get past the pain. It crippled them emotionally because they were never able to get free. They were enslaved by that moment.

They continued to live out the experience in their minds, constantly making it real and relevant. They rehearsed the pain continuously until it absorbed them. From this point, the villains made it their lifes' mission to cause others the same pain or even worse, and perpetuate their misery onto others.

Subliminally are you a villain? Does this describe you at all in any way? The first step to freedom is honesty.

The process called forgiveness is a difficult one because it defies human nature. It feels good to be angry. It brings certainty. While you can stay angry, it also is a perfect recipe for being alone. Being in this state is not attractive and you are literally blocking your blessings.

There are three powerful steps to forgive that one must take in order to possess their freedom:

Decide to forgive. This is something that has to be said out loud more than once and don't kid yourself. The feeling of hate will return immediately when you see the person who hurt you. This is where perspective comes in. The warring feelings that arise within you are natural; that's why I say this is a process. Just because you have stated that you do sincerely forgive, does not mean that anger does not arrive. Allow yourself to acknowledge those feelings without letting them dominate you.

Pray for them. Pray out loud, specifically, God's blessing on them. I know it sounds crazy and you will recognize how difficult this is at first. However, this process is twofold. One, it is hard to hold hatred when you pray for someone, unless you're praying wrath. And two, it destroys bitterness because you are going against your nature. This process is more for you than it is them. God will deal with them. Don't do His job; Vengeance is His, not yours. God cannot bless you with hostility in your heart. The brain can only deal with one thought at a time. You don't have room for harboring that. This means simply, "I'm not going to dwell on dead issues of the past. My time and future are too important."

Future focus: STOP talking about past issues. Since the brain can only focus on one thing at a time, start with your future and how you are going to get better. This is where your vision comes in. If you don't have one, get a vision for yourself quickly. Put it on your wall. This way, you will be able to see it every day. This anchors your mind for success because our visual surroundings enter our subconscious minds. We outwardly express them from there. You must be intentional about your purpose. Write down your bucket list of life. Don't wait until you get old, for you may never see old age. There is a massive power in now. If you do these things, forgiveness is complete and it will revolutionize your life.

Is there anyone whom you need to forgive?

_____
_____
_____
_____
_____
_____
_____
_____

Day #11

Day #11
Knock, Knock …

"Guard your heart, for out it flows the issues of life."
– Proverbs 4:23

"Knock, knock?"

"Who's there?"

"It's us," the media replies, "But we're already in. You see, we have studied the psychology of the mind and we have found that there are several ways to win over the attitudes of people. One is that we understand that it takes some 'No's' to get one 'Yes.'

Therefore, we bombard you with the same product and services until you say, 'Yes.' Another is that we limit your choices. Research shows that fifty percent of how we learn is by what we see and hear. This means that if we keep showing you highlights of the same message with catchy phrases and music along with attractive people, it is inevitable that you'll buy. So, if we have control over your eye and ear gate via TV, this gives us incredible access to infiltrate sound doctrine and thinking.

While we can't control anybody's behavior, we do know that we can influence it. The power of suggestion goes very far. Do you really think we will spend $300,000 on a thirty-second commercial to only make you smile and be happy? No! You're not that important. But, we know what our agenda is and we know that spending some time and money to manipulate your mind will give us huge dividends in return and will keep a lot of loyal customers for a long time because most people don't renew their mind. People look to television for escape from their current pain, which means that they don't want to think. We can accomodate that at a monthly cost."

The Solution: Good knowledge. People are destroyed for a lack of knowledge, and because they reject good knowledge when they get it.

It is vital to understand that lazy thinking brings your defenses down. In contrast, diligent thinkers are not easily fooled. You must protect the doorways to your heart, which are your ears; your eyes and your mouth. This means that we must watch the things that we hear, see, and say.

There are dark forces that have gotten much more aggressive over the years, so Christians can't afford to be lazy in their behavior and in what they allow themselves to watch and to say. Many have been defeated by their own words.

More now than ever we must pray for discernment because the devil is subtle. Forsake not the assembly of the saints and read the Bible for daily encouragement. Accompany yourself with mature believers and not gossipers.

What you don't know, ask someone. According to *American psychiatrist, Dr. William Glasser, fifty percent of what we learn is by what we see and hear*. It could make the difference between emotional poverty and spiritual maturity. Become doers and not just hearers of the Word of God. Know that this spiritual fight is a good one, worthy of discipline and good action.

Jesus has already won the battle for us, but we must do our part. Remember, God is able to do exceeding, abundantly above all we can ask or think, according to the power that works within us. Let us work that power.

Day #12

Day #12

Understanding Your Value

*"Wise women see things as they are,
not as their low self-esteem allows."*

– Sharon L. Alder

*"Sincerity makes the least person to be of more value than
the most talented hypocrite."*

– Charles Spurgeon

I told a coworker that a doctor said that it is not good to eat while standing. To which she asked, "Who said that?" I responded I didn't know and then said, "You don't know who I am, I don't just say anything and I'm not going to prove it to you."

At some point, especially as you get older, you

have to know who you are; your worth and what you bring to the table. It has to go beyond things, money, and where you graduated from. Those things mean very little if your character sucks.

Not putting a limit on what anyone does for work because it can contribute massively to others in a way that is wonderful. But if one's confidence is in the fact that he is a doctor and treats his wife like crap because she is a housewife, then he is lacking love and understanding and without those you are not much.

Arthur C. Clarke said, "It has yet to be proven that intelligence has any survival value." Comparing is not wise because it undermines what the other has to offer. When the scientist, doctor, or accountant are stressed, they seek out enjoyment and relief. Therefore, they seek entertainment or get a great massage from people like me. My value as a Massage Therapist is incomparable. If you don't think so, get a massage.

One of the reasons why relationships and marriages are not working is because we are competing instead of appreciating. We are not created equal. Man cannot do what a woman does and vice versa. This is the whole basis of attraction.

If we compete, we lose love. If we appreciate, the possibilities are endless. When we seek to appreciate another's differences, we gain from the wonder of it and the person. We don't have to fully understand. If we value them, the person will stay, if not they leave.

Even Jesus said, "Do not cast your pearls before swine." Another way of putting that is what Michael Bassey Johnson observed, "Do not share your thoughts with people who think that what you are thinking about is not worth thinking." Depending on your station in life, this may take you some time to sort out and that's okay. But get there because you will waste your time, energy, and words if you don't.

Understanding your value means knowing who you are. It means that everyone is not for you and that is perfect. You don't need everyone. The most famous people don't have all the followers in the world. What is for you is for you. Stop fighting for everyone's love and admiration.

Sharon L. Alder stated, "Wise women see things as they are, not as their low self-esteem allows." Your self-worth sees things either poorly or greatly. This comes from your inner self.

A woman said to me once, "I could tell you have a good soul when I looked into your eyes." Wow! What a compliment. If people refuse to see your greatness, then they are simply not worth your precious time.

I have learned the powerful lesson of simply being. The older I get, the less I say. I work very hard on who I want to be and watch greatness flock to me. When people know your worth, they treat you as such. It may take some time but trust me, it is a journey worth taking.

Do you know your value?
Name some qualities that make you valuable.

"People will walk in and out of your life,
but the one whose footstep made a
long-lasting impression is the one you should
never allow to walk out.

– Michael Bassey Johnson

Day #13

Day #13
Maybe You Should
Shut Up This Time

.⌒ ■ ⌒.

"Think twice and say nothing."
– Chinese Proverb

Oh, the places we can go if we can just shut our mouths. It is amazing how much we can learn if we harness the power of self-control to not defend ourselves in certain arguments. The drama would dissipate almost instantaneously.

And it's not like we haven't done it before. We've done so in places like the workforce with our bosses or managers or when we are being pulled over by a police officer. We choose the people to mouth off at for various reasons. One is because we know we can win the argument or take advantage of them due to the fact that we are savvy with our verbiage.

But what does this contribute emotionally and what kind of atmosphere are we bringing when we do this? Doing this regularly provides a habit of selfishness and causes us to miss the bigger picture.

The Chinese Proverb, "Think twice and say nothing," is monumental and will change your life if you apply it. I personally have learned so much by saying nothing and being still. When this proverb is applied, it gives the inner genius in you room to breathe. You get to see things you've never seen, and hear things that are refreshing to your spirit.

Most people don't slow down and quiet themselves enough to hear the new.

You cancel out this greatness if you always have to defend yourself. Why? Because the brain can only deal with one sensation or thought at a time.

You cannot allow your feelings to be so important that you miss out on new revelation. The key phrase to this Chinese proverb is, "Think twice." Notice that it didn't say, "Think once." The second time of thinking gives the brain a chance to slow down and to examine better possibilities. This is where genius comes in because the greatest things come to those who think.

"Maybe You Should Shut Up This Time" is simply a challenge to think greater than you are used to and to say nothing so that you can see the difference that being quiet will make in every aspect of your life. The Book of Proverbs says, "The mouth of a fool invites him a beating." By me applying this principle, I have escaped fist fights; arguments; chaos; and all kinds of drama.

In contrast, by applying this, I've also written books; articles; had the boldness to speak to beautiful women; and have gained so much peace in my life. The blessings are numerous and definitely outweigh the normality of speaking too much.

If you want to get out of the average way of doing things, this is one way. When you speak less and observe more, you open up doors of enlightenment. I promise you, this path is a much better one and it will improve your life a thousand times over.

Day #14

Day #14
Tears

Tears are very beautiful,
even when cried in pain
They are like drops of healing waters,
they are sweet like summer rain.
When tears roll down my face,
they let me know I'm real
They teach me about expression,
they embrace the way that I feel.

Tears are not sadness,
that are cried by girls and boys,
They are reminders of our past and future
Our failures, our triumphs and joys.
Tears evoke emotion, that touch the lives of men,
They pierce the hearts of women and make us
understand.
In life there are many lessons and none that we
should fear,
And the one that I am learning, is never hold
back your tears.

Jopala poetry

Men's Cry

So many times I needed comfort,
instead I got complaints,
So many times I needed to be held,
instead you just refrained.
It feels like we as men are supposed to shut up
As the unbearable volume of life
turns up our pain,
Like teenagers we get recognized
when we do something wrong.
When violent outburst and anger rises,
the media sing our song.
So, Lord, we have to turn to you
because our women pass us by,
They see our pain and then refrain, so alone, we
sit and cry.

When was the last time you have cried?

How do you view crying?

Day #15

Day #15
Failure Is An Option!

*The greatest mistake you can make in life is
continually to be fearing you will make one.*
                                    - Elbert Hubbard

Who wouldn't depend on Michael Jordan to make the
last shot with only three seconds on the clock to win
a Championship game? What you may not know was
that he has missed six thousand shots. Luther Vandross
was booed off the Apollo stage three times. Winston
Churchill failed the sixth grade and Albert Einstein
couldn't speak until he was four and couldn't read
until he was nine.

Henry Ford went bankrupt two times before he built

the Ford Company. Yet we don't remember them for their failures because it was these things that propelled them to be some of the greatest minds ever. Babe Ruth struck out more than anyone in history, but he also scored more home runs than anyone in history.

If you're paying attention and have the right perspective, failure is not only inevitable in life, but it is one of your greatest assets. Failure is there to teach you how to not repeat failure; how not to be cowardly; how not to give up. The cleaning solution was named "401," because after four-hundred failures they finally got it right. Now, that's a champion.

Unfortunately our society quickly encourages us to give up instead of think. The greatest minds think and rethink until they produce success. You don't get what you deserve, you get what you work for, and then-you deserve it.

Once you get this outlook on life, things become so much easier because you are respecting process. There is nothing new under the sun. People get into trouble because they are attempting to reinvent the wheel instead of learning and then working what they've learned.

Marvin Winans wrote a song that said, "Bring back the days of 'Yeah and Nay.'" I heard somebody say that God wasn't going to do that. If that's the case, then we are lost forever because we cannot abandon what our forefathers did; skip life's classes and expect to succeed.

Failure is a part of life and wise people accept that. The great news is that we can expedite our success rate by learning from those whom have gone before us.

Clarence Day said, "Information's pretty thin stuff unless mixed with experience." The same principles of success apply in life but the styles have changed, that's all. Don't be afraid to fail. What you should be afraid of is not trying and staying in a cage of should have; could have been. Those fears are for cowards, not for champions.

We are God's people. We are champions. It is fear that teaches us to fear failure. God has not given us a spirit of fear, but He has given unto us a spirit of power, a spirit of love and self-discipline. With that in mind, what would you do if you knew you couldn't fail?

Day #16

Day #16
Kid Power

.⌐ ■ ⌐.

"I tell you the truth,
anyone who will not receive the kingdom of God
like a little child, will never enter it."

Luke 18:17

Kids are absolutely incredible. Their energy; smiles; honesty; potential; ability to learn and observe; and their joyous and infectious laughter is contagious. It is vital that we see their purity and glean from them. When they enter a room, they demand smiles and immediately force us to reconsider our posture, language, and attitude. They are powerful reminders of what many adults have lost: the ability to enjoy life, worry free.

We as parents know firsthand the joys of having them. Who else runs to us with massive smiles calling our names? Who else can remind us to be open and honest about our feelings? Who shows us to live life without fear? Children. They are an amazing gift to us that we should never forget.

Jesus said that if we don't have childlike faith, we will not see heaven. I heard a preacher say that God's greatest pleasure is to be believed and that His greatest pain is to be doubted. Children trust. They are not bogged down with fear, bills or responsibilities that take up mental space and energy. Unfortunately though we teach them that by our actions as they get older. The reason we should learn from children is because everything comes down to what we believe. Many miracles were performed because people simply believed. God will not move in our lives if we don't believe.

Here are some powerful things that children teach us:

Humility - We can't use impressive vocabulary with children because they will look at us like we are crazy. This is good because children force us to come out of our selfish world and make things simple. Everything is upfront and simple for kids - the way life really should be. We as adults often complicate many things.

Honesty - Children teach us to be honest. When things are honest, they are pure; right; and easy. In contrast, when they are the opposite, it's messy. Have you ever noticed that children will say anything that comes to mind? That speaks of freedom and living without fear.

Fun - If there is anything kids know how to do is have a good time. I've recently gone to the park with my daughter and went on the slide and swings. It was liberating. These things are priceless.

When life gets tumultuous, and it will, children teach us not to take life so seriously. At the end of life, we want to enter into heaven, so let's have childlike faith and have fun. Let us learn from the kids because kids have power.

"Consider what I say; and the Lord give thee
understanding in all things."

2 Timothy 1:7 (KJV)

Are you teachable/humble?

_____
_____
_____
_____

Are you holding bitterness or resentment toward
another?

_____
_____
_____
_____

Do you forgive quickly?

_____
_____
_____
_____

Day #17

Day #17
The Best Sex

.⌐ ■ ⌐.

"Entreat me not to leave you . . ."
Ruth 1:16

Contrary to what most people think, the best sex goes beyond the physical. The best sex is emotional and consists of these three components: care, compromise, and connection. The deeper these emotions are felt toward each other, the better the sex.

In this day, this is important to realize because the days of quickies and hookups are becoming more seldom. People are looking for the real thing. I have found it interesting to hear young women say to me that they are celibate.

Care: How much do you care for the person? When you truly care for someone, you want to please them physically and in every way. You are attentive to their needs and you don't mind going the extra mile to make sure they're happy. It brings you pleasure to see them smile. When a person truly cares for you, sex is fulfilling because it originates from a deep place of love and this love gives on a level that is beautiful and unconditional. It searches to please because of the care that is attached to it.

Compromise: There is no room for domination when love is involved. One must compromise until there is a win-win situation that benefits both parties. Love does not dominate or control, it influences. With compromise, it kills off selfishness. This enhances the care factor and empowers both to be free. When freedom comes, sex is better because you are more creative, and you feel safety with communicating new things and going on new adventures.

Connection: There are some women I have had to run from because the attraction was so deep that I knew if we were to hook up with each other, it would be amazing and addictive. However, for the marriage union, this is what you want. You want the kind of connection that flourishes. When you have that kind of connection, you become inseparable because your love for each other has stood the test of time and chaos.

If sex is just physical, it will fade with infatuation. And most of us know how fast that fades. We want more than thirty days of lust. We want care, comfort, connection, and someone who will compromise. We get these things and our sex lives will thrive. Marilyn Monroe stated, "We are all sexual creatures, thank God, but it's a pity so many people despise and crush this natural gift." Well said and so true. If you despise it, after a while it becomes a meaningless pleasure. But if you honor it, it will become a longing fulfilled.

How do you view sex?

What does it mean to you?

Day #18

Day #18
The Questions

.⌒ ■ ⌒.

"You have no right to an answer for a question that you haven't asked."

– Dr. Mike Murdock

What do I want? This is the ultimate question that one should ask themselves about life. But be sure not to give the superficial answers that most give. You know – happiness; a great marriage; kids; and nice house, etc. In the words of the rapper Dr. Dre, "I just wanna be successful." T.K. Harv. Eker states that, "Most people don't get what they want because they don't know what they want." He was speaking specifically about finances but it applies to every aspect of life.

Your wants cannot just be driven by shallow desire, but by a deeper sense of purpose and a knowledge that comes with counting the cost.

Over half of the marriages in the US end in divorce. Thirty percent of now divorced women knew at the time of marriage that it was wrong but did it anyway. Why? Because their wants were not connected to their needs. When your wants are not aligned with your needs you make immature decisions that are shallow and they do not last because they carried no depth or weight.

Why do I want it? This speaks to your reason. I love this question because the "why" is the driving motivation behind everything we do. This is where that first deep heart answer comes that if we don't like it, we ignore it and choose the other voice because we don't want to admit the ugly. You know, like getting with a person just because you wanted to sleep with him or her or getting married because you want a child now before you get too old.

The "why" reveals where our true motives are. If the motive is not pure, this is where God can clean up our hearts and the surgery that is needed can be performed if we let Him in. But when we stay in control, things get messy because we were not honest with our original intent.

Most people are running from themselves and they are using the things, relationships and success as masks. There's nothing wrong with wanting the finer things in life and sharing them with that special someone. But when those desires are out of priority, then things get messy.

What are you going to do? This is where the plan of being diligent comes in. This can be a lot of fun if you have the right perspective. Too many people allow their pursuit of goals to become arduous. Not saying that they're not but life is about the lessons.

Treasure everything! It is truly the challenging times that lead you to greatness, if one doesn't give up. The more detailed your plan is in achieving your goals, the more likely you will achieve them. Start with small dreams and then build big. And if you do it with passion, then you can follow the words of Mike Tyson, "I'm a dreamer. I have to dream and reach for the stars, and if I miss a star then I grab a handful of clouds." Go get 'em!

Day #19

Day #19
GREATNESS:
Pre-Approved

.(■ (.

*"The greatest truth that must be recognized is that
in every child, every man lays the potential for greatness."*

– Robert Kennedy

On behalf of Keeping It Real Ministries, we are
delighted to let you know that you have been
preapproved for Greatness. The Heavenly Father
has seen you and sent His Son to cancel all previous,
present, and future sins that would impede your
amazing destiny. Because of the finished work of
Calvary, you qualify for an unlimited credit line of

love, joy, peace, and prosperity in every area of life at zero percent interest.

This is not a gimmick and there are no hidden fees. Please do not ignore this letter. There are too many people who are not using the incredible access that God has already provided for them. And when Christians do this especially, it makes the angels cry because it's like they are crucifying Christ all over again.

The Bible has made it very clear of His abounding love and blessings for us. In Daniel, He said, "Those who know their God shall do great exploits." In Proverbs, He said, "The blessing of the Lord makes you rich and adds no sorrow to it." In Psalms He said, "Wealth and riches shall be in the house of the righteous and your children will be mighty in the land." In John He said, "He wishes that we prosper and be in good health in all things just as our soul prospers," and that "greater is He that is in us than he that is in all the world."

When you can begin to understand the countless benefits that you have in the Scriptures, then you will live an amazing life. But you cannot live out what you do not understand. It is the reason why Solomon said,

"In all your getting, get understanding.

The purpose of this letter Beloved is to simply remind you of the access you have. Many of you are stressed; not getting along with your spouses; some of your children are unruly; and your finances are out of control. Yet I said there remains a rest for the people of God and that I came so that we would have life and have it more abundantly.

My dear children, you don't need abundant life in heaven, you need it on earth. I cannot force you to take what has already been provided for you, so I sent one of my oracles to simply remind you to cast your cares upon Me because I care for you. To seek first the kingdom of God and His righteousness and all other things will be added to you. To bring the tithes and offerings into your churches and if you do, I will open the windows of heaven and pour you out a blessing that you cannot receive. So, don't let your heart be troubled, have faith, and be happy because you have been preapproved for greatness.

Do you believe that you have greatness in you?

From this day forward, how can you begin to release it?

Day #20

Day #20

Hypocritical Politeness

.⸜■⸝.

"There are three things in the world that deserve no mercy:
hypocrisy, fraud, and tyranny."

– *Frederick William Robertson*

On November 8th, 2016 Donald J. Trump was elected the forty-fifth President of the United States, which shocked and upset millions. People were marching with chants screaming, "Not my President," and there were women demanding that they be respected. A nation in shock with even commentators stating, "We don't know what he's going to do."

Violence erupted in some parts of the country and racial tension was high. People were saying things like, "Racism is back" to which I replied on my show, "It never left."

America has done the unfortunate job of burying lies and greatness for years. This is obvious with slavery. This country was built off the backs of slaves. Many inventions were stolen and overlooked because people refused to change for the betterment of all.

I thought, like many, that Christopher Columbus discovered America because that's what we were taught. Now we are in the Information Age, where freedom is supposedly supreme. But we have black men being shot to death who are unarmed while whites kill many and are apprehended without a bruise. That's not interesting. That's straight hypocrisy and appalling.

So now we have social media, where everyone is an immediate star and their opinion is valid and important. It is interesting the see the news commentators bombard us with the need for gun control only when whites die by their own hands, but not blacks being killed by police officers who are not punished for doing so. We don't need gun control, we need character building. Gun control is a fancy term to push Martial Law so that no one has guns but the state.

To blame killings on mental illness and being lost is incorrect. The reason I know this is because I was diagnosed with Bipolar Disorder and have had nine mental breakdowns. I know full well of being out of my mind, but I haven't killed anyone. But on a real bad day, I might give you the finger.

Tennessee Williams observed, "The only thing worse than a liar is a liar that's a hypocrite." I am not sure if lies and hypocrisy will stop, especially when it is coming from government and some of our most powerful leaders.

The solution has to be God in America again. You can't take prayer out of schools; take Christ out of Christmas; and water down anything that has to do with the name of Jesus and expect our nation to succeed morally. It's impossible. My prayer and hope contain two things: one, that people who continue to refuse God and not let Him in their hearts to govern, would accept personal responsibility for the chaos and a nation out of control. Second, that we would accept Christ in our lives so that we can live in peace, harmony and love for our fellow man. I'm David Carruthers, for The House of David, and I approve this message.

Day #21

Day#21
Stolen Waters

.⌒ ■ ⌒.

"Your limits are liars. Your fears are thieves"
– Robin Sharma

There is something exhilarating about taking that which is not yours. It is invigorating. The forbidden is sweet because it's off limits and now in your possession. This provides a sensation that is quite like no other, because for the thief, it is about seizing an opportunity that is against ethical and moral code.

All thieves like to break the rules and justify that which is wrong. One proverb states, "He who holds the ladder is as bad as the thief." The mind that is not renewed plays life on a dangerous edge, only to ignorantly find out that destruction is soon waiting. For some, the act of getting caught causes them to become meticulous at conniving, which leads them down a very destructive path.

"Stolen waters" is much more than stealing. It's about manipulation and allowing someone to believe a lie that isn't true. Thirty percent of divorced women knew at the time they got married, that the marriage was wrong, or "stolen waters."[4]

Every 98 seconds, another American is sexually assaulted[5] – "stolen waters." The effects of "stolen waters"are too numerous to write about in this devotional. The good news is that Jesus loves you dearly and will not hold these sins against you if you come to Him and change. To attempt to change on your own is near futile because you will be fighting your own nature.

Allow God to change you by renewing your mind with His word. Many do not attempt this because they see the process as too arduous. But don't allow the

---

[4]   https://www.marieclaire.com/sex-love/advice/a5998/married-wrong-husband/

[5]   www.rainn.org/statistics

enemy of your soul to keep you in fear and believing that you have to be in bondage to behavior that is toxic.

It is a lie and lies are limits and fears are thieves. Be set free by the power of God. He is not judging you, He loves you. This moment can be a call to action to change your destiny into the person whom you know you can be and more.

Most of us know that we are more than what we have become, but unfortunately most don't become it. The process of change is actually more glorious than the change itself because you can later teach others to do the same.

The problem with "stolen waters" is that they are stolen. Why steal, when God has given you the ability to create? If you allow God to elevate your thinking, then greatness is inevitable. As Les Brown said, "The problem is not that we think too high and miss it, but rather that we think too low and hit it." The Almighty God has given you a wonderful invitation. I hope that you accept it.

Day #22

Day #22

Suicide Is Never The Answer

.⌒ ■ ⌒.

"Do you really want to die?
No one commits suicide because they want to die.
Then why do it?
Because they want to stop the pain"

- Tiffanie DeBartolo

The pain does stop. I can promise you that. As one who has been suicidal a few times, the pain goes away. Some pain you do have to manage. What you need is not necessary to stop feeling because that would be death. You need a fresh perspective and that, my friend, is life.

Jesus loves you more than you'll ever know. I had absolutely no plans to put this entry in here but this day I felt a strong sense that I should. Pain sucks. You may doubt this, but joy does come again.

This is where you have to take life one day at a time. Be grateful for life in the midst of the chaos. It doesn't last always. Most people look at greatness as the big picture. But it is in times of extreme chaos and turmoil, they find out that they have incredible strength. And so do you.

Tomorrow may not be that much better but it will be better than today, if you change your focus. I recall living in the mental institution and felt like the days were an eternity. And yet, slowly but surely, I got better. A visit from family members and friends breathed new life into me. A smile from someone who had it just as bad as me on the ward - we are talking – hey, that's a new friend. If you look harder, you will find things to smile about. Remember your talents and you will see hope.

One of the mistakes being in a suicidal state is that one concentrates on negative voices and discounts what one does well as ordinary. Nonsense! What you do well is great and there are people waiting in the world for you to take your place. Who would have thought I who was suicidal am now writing to you in one of my books to say to you that you matter; you can make it; and you are loved.

See how things turn around? There is greatness in you. That is something you should say out loud every day until you get used to you saying it and start feeling it. While the world is not a nice place to live sometimes, I'm thinking it will be a lot better with you.

Day #23

Day #23

The Enemy Within

"If there is no enemy within,
the enemy outside can do us no harm."

– African Proverb

The beautiful thing about getting older is that you begin to see the same things over and over again. If you're paying attention, this can put you on the road to mastery in an area in which you closely observe and constantly practice. In contrast, the sad thing about getting older is that you see the same things over and over again. It is amazing how so many people are running from their own pain thinking that if they ignore it, it will go away.

Pain and issues never go away until you deal with them. They are like car tickets that gain interest and max out after a certain time. I have seen people die of old age and not live out their potential because they covered their pain with pride and pleasure. This resulted in broken relationships never being restored because of the issues that were never mastered. It is a sad way to live life when you conquer so many things, but never yourself.

Greatness comes from within and so does poverty. I heard a college football coach say "Greatness does not get along with mediocrity and mediocrity doesn't get along with greatness." Many of us have seen shows of some of the greatest stars who have achieved unbelievable heights refuse to gain control over the demons that were in their own minds.

This has become the theme of America: to obtain great accomplishments but have poor character. The best way to fix what is happening on the inside is Jesus. There is unlimited power and love in that name. But one will never know this unless they give Him a sincere try.

It baffles me why people don't run to Him. Many

have not, I believe, because they have seen so much hypocrisy in some Christians that they align that to God. But you must remember, people will be people and with their best efforts at times will let you down. Not God. He is amazing and will deal appropriately with the issues of your broken heart.

The reason why this is so vital is because when people are broken, they do broken things and hurt others around them. It is inevitable. However, when you are healed, full of love, kindness and cheer, then you spread that and your influence grows positively. I've seen good people become unstoppable, not because they're perfect but because they're heart is whole.

One must unclog the clutter if there is going to be a beautiful flow. It's like alkaline water that flushes the body. The same must be done for the emotions. Please don't be afraid of the process. The beauty is there because that's where you learn the lessons. Most people don't finish their process and never see their true beauty. The grass is truly greener on the other side but that grass is only greener if you water it. Your greatness awaits but, you must first deal with the enemy within, so the enemy outside can do you no harm.

Day #24

Day #24
Letter Of Resignation

"The safest road to hell is the gradual one–the gentle slope, soft underfoot, without sudden turnings, without milestones, without signpost."

– C.S. Lewis

To Whom It May Concern:

We are writing this letter because our time is almost up. There are some who are beginning to pay attention and figure out our schemes, plots and lies. People are realizing that the government is corrupt and that the rules and regulations are not profiting the middle class, just the rich.

We have created a dynamic in which people are

working twice as hard for the same benefits they had a decade ago. Our efforts have produced the crash of real estate and Wall Street, the destruction of 9/11 and have masterminded the highest jail population in the world. We also have produced millions of dysfunctional families and the breakdown of the family structure.

One of the reasons for our success is that we send distractions so that Christians do not pray. Most of those fools fall for it.

The ethics and morality of this nation is at an all-time low and we are very proud of that. Our goal is to continue to quiet the Christians so that they will be partial to the secular movement because we know that evil exists when good people do nothing about it. We have been able to increase violence and pornography that we have created via influence of the media; the dehumanizing of leaders and the suicides of pastors and we realize that we must increase our presence to produce a lack of hope because there are too many people waking up.

We are hearing stories of Christians beginning to pray and fast for the healing of the land. This is not good because what we have found is that we are powerless against a praying Church and a people who truly believe and implement the Word of God. Some of us have even gone back to our chief and begged him to take us out of the fight because of this powerful, relentless Remnant.

We know we can't win against Christians who know who they are.

However, before you get happy and begin your dancing, we should let you know that we will not stop until that dreadful day of Christ's return. We will do everything in our power to kill, to steal, and to destroy all Christians and people who are not on our side. We will study your every weakness and attack them. For some, this means your children, because we know that they are defenseless and ignorant. We thrive off people not knowing and educating themselves.

Our goal is simple: to deceive as many people as possible and offer them a lifetime of earthly pleasure in exchange for an eternity of pain; torment; aguish and darkness.

Sincerely,

The Devil's Advocates

Day #25

Day #25

The Invitations

"Two roads diverged in the woods, and I took the one less traveled by and that has made all the difference."

– Robert Frost

"Please allow me to introduce the characteristics of myself. I won't say my name because that may cause the invitation to be less appealing. I am filled with love, joy, peace, wisdom and in these you are guaranteed to get the fullness of everything you need in life. No gimmicks, no tricks or lies - straight up. Everything that comes from me is pure and original.

After a little while, you will be required to apply what you have heard so that you can enjoy the benefits of membership, including discipline; prudence; learning and the denying of oneself.

What I will tell you is this: while some of these things will be very difficult at the onset, your rewards will far outweigh any trouble or trial that will ultimately come. Also, you can terminate this contract at any time and can come back to me any time and we can continue where we left off because I value choice.

My name is Jesus Christ. I died for your sins so that you can experience abundant life here on earth and everlasting life which is paradise in heaven."

"Okay, so he had his turn and now it is mine. Let me tell you my characteristics. My deal is filled with pleasure; good times; sex; partying and the ability to do whatever you want to do. Life is about being free and enjoying the moments. My plan doesn't come with these contingencies of discipline and all that crap. That's too much work.

I guarantee you success and everything that you need to make it in life, which is money. Look at the economy with people struggling. They're unhappy because they don't have money. I can give you luxury so that you never have to worry about those things again.

Now, there is a price but don't worry about it, just sign and we'll get to that later. Here's a couple of grand just for good measure for your signing."

Unfortunately, most people get caught up in the latter plan. What the second person didn't tell you is that he is the devil and his price is your soul which means that you will be tormented with excruciating pain forever in exchange for this lifetime of pleasure and rejecting Jesus Christ. What he doesn't tell you is that he is the master of deception. He is known as the father of lies and he uses diversions filled with pleasures to get you off course to that which really matters.

Jesus said in Matthew 7:13, "Many will enter in the wide gate that leads to destruction but few find the gate that leads to eternal life." Choose the first option and listen to the wisdom of Robert Frost who said, "Two roads diverged in the woods and I took the one less traveled by, and that has made all the difference."

Day #26

Day# 26

Death Of A Lady

And now the categories for best female in a man's role are, "Scandal;" "Atomic Blonde;" "Proud Mary;" "Lady Killers;" "Wanted;" and "Queen of the South." "And the winner is . . ."

Do you get where I'm going here? The very first thing powerful people do when they want to make something popular and accepted is put it on the big screen because fifty percent of what we learn is by what we see and hear.[6] The media has massive power. You rarely see women in the role of a loving supporting wife. We don't see nurturers and mothers who keep the family together. Women's liberation was created in 1965 and evolved from equality to female domination.

Right now, I sound like the guy who is trying to put women back in aprons full time. But someone has to address the fact that we have more singles now than ever before in history; marriage is continually on the decline; and divorce is steadily going up. I'm not blaming this on women but I am saying that more men are saying things like, "They want to be men," or "They don't listen," or "She thinks I want her money" and "These hoes ain't loyal," to list a few.

It was Jackie Kennedy who said it best, "I'll be a wife and mother first, then First Lady." Most today want to be a First Lady. Our television reality shows the opposite, including women who don't know how to reason. They will fight you in a hot second, swear like a sailor but have a body like a goddess. Jimmy Evans stated it best, "When a culture becomes inwardly depraved, they become outwardly focused."

---

[6]   https://inclued.wordpress.com/2011/05/25/we-learn-10-of-is-this-true-where-does-it-all-come-from/

So honestly, why am I doing this? Why would I write such material and potentially offend many women? Mae West said it perfectly: "When women go wrong, men go right after them." I clearly understand that many will not listen in this day but some will and those are the ones whom I'm after. I write this because a woman's power and worth are not in competing with men or trying to outperform her man. That's not intelligent. We're on the same team.

A real woman supports; nurtures; listens intently; and produces powerful change that benefits everyone around her. She doesn't put her children before her man because he gave her the children. She isn't out of order.

Her presence is incredible and moving. I love what Anais Nin says, "I, with a deeper instinct, choose a man who compels my strength, who makes enormous demands on me, who does not doubt my courage or my toughness, who does not believe me naïve or innocent, who has the courage to treat me like a woman." Is there anything more that needs to be said of her power? A woman like that a man will not leave and if he does, his manhood is questionable.

My prayer is the return of the Lady would be evident across the nation despite what the media is trying to have her pursue. That women would be steadfast and sure on what their purpose is.

It will be evident when you walk into a room. It is not just your body that men are looking at, but your presence and character. Let it be said that your inner beauty is so compelling that we will see what Sydney Biddle Barrows observed, "The more you act like a lady, the more he'll act like a gentleman."

Day #27

Day#27

Chasing The Delusion

"Do not try to bend the spoon, that's impossible,
instead only try to see the truth . . . there is no spoon . . .
Then you'll see it is not the spoon that bends but yourself."

– *The Matrix*

My perfect woman is about 5'6, with an hourglass body, and the beauty of Halle Berry but with a darker complexion. She's a prayer warrior, loves to cook and do all the things I love to do and is massively attentive to my needs. Here's the problem: she doesn't exist. There are so many people that run after success eluding the very thing that they are chasing after.

We must be very careful because God gives us

amazing opportunities, but we can fail to see them if we have a preexisting view of what it already looks like and can miss the real thing. I honestly believe everyone gets a couple of chances to get Mr. or Mrs. Right. You don't get eight. It is vital that we begin to get over our image and deal with reality. This means being very cognizant of your weaknesses and the baggage that you bring to a relationship. There are too many people who have sky expectations but only give on a valley level.

People who chase delusions are actually in pain, thus the reason for the chase. They feel that if they amass certain things and prestige, they will be successful and it will dull the pain. But that is a temporary fix. This usually backfires because it plunges you further into the delusion. So, when it resurfaces, it comes back harder. This means you actually create more pain by not dealing with the previous pain.

Delusional people also have a tendency to lie. They do this to protect their images, which covers up their weaknesses. One of the biggest problems with chasing delusions is that it's a pursuit of a never-ending lie and you don't deal with the giant within. As Carl Jung said, "He who looks outside dreams, he who looks inside awakens."

God has no problem giving us an abundance of things, but His kingdom has to be priority. In the book of James, it talks about asking for blessings and not getting them because the motives were wrong. God is big on motives. He will not give you things if that's how you identify success instead of with Him.

Tye Tribbett sings a beautiful song on his album, Stand Up, entitled "Chasing after You." This song speaks about falling in love with Jesus. I never thought that I would be in a place where I was excited about God and wanting to know Him more. It's an amazing thing. He really is a relational God who desires to give us more than we can ask or think. I pray that whatever ails you or is trying to put you in a state of delusion, would be diminished so that you can know the fullness of God's glory and the beauty of His presence. He has already chased us. Now it's our turn to chase Him.

Day #28

Day#28
Members Only

*"It isn't my responsibility to judge outsiders,
but it certainly is your responsibility to
judge those inside the church who are sinning."*

1 Corinthians 5:12

"There will be a meeting for members only after church immediately after the 11 AM service. Now what I have to say is vitally important. It was brought to my attention that Jack and Tina Johnson, members and leaders of this church, have filed for divorce. I, as their pastor was deeply hurt because I had no idea that they were having marital issues. I have preached several times about accountability, honesty, and not giving the devil an inch because he will take a mile.

I honestly felt betrayed because we have provided so much powerful information through books, audio CDs, DVDs, seminars and have paid top marriage professionals from across the country to teach us, and to still have this outcome is confusing. Marriage is a sacred covenant that is supposed to be cherished over a lifetime. To share your intimate problems with heathens and unbelievers in a court system designed for the destruction of unity and the building of evil empires, is preposterous. Therefore, the purpose of this meeting is to set some new guidelines concerning the members of this church.

From now on all associate pastors; leaders; elders; and deacons who are married will be assigned two to five married couples for them to mentor. We cannot prevent failure and manage crisis in people's lives if we have no idea what is going on with them. The day for "I don't want anyone in my business" is over. I have no desire to lead a church whose divorce rate is just as high as in the world.

We have to get to a place in our thinking that divorce is not an option. The Apostle Paul talked about growing unto maturity and how discord, jealousy, and not being able to get along should not be amongst

God's people. Are we not God's people? We have to do better. I believe at this point we should go back to Wednesday night cell groups. We had a stronger church when this was in place. People were growing and there was much more accountability.

Finally, we have to teach people how to pray and how to do spiritual warfare. I've received too many phone calls about issues that the saints should be handling themselves. My fear is that people are hearing but not listening. It is vital beloved, that in all of your getting, you get an understanding of what you are hearing. Otherwise you will be coming to church Sunday after Sunday, year after year, staying the same with no power.

We have to be about results. The Church is not the building. You are the Church. Remember Jesus told Peter, "Upon this rock, will I build my Church." The name Peter means "The Rock."

Saints, let us increase our vitality to live for God. These are the last days. We must remember that we will be judged for every word, action and thought. The devil is not going to let up, and as God's chosen people, neither are we. We can do all things through

Christ who strengthens us.

This is the good fight of faith but remember, it is a fight. Remember that we have been promised the victory but we have to earn it.

God bless you Saints. Go in the peace of God.

Now unto Him who is able to keep you from falling and present you before his glorious presence without fault and great joy. To the only God and Savior be glory, majesty, power and authority through Jesus Christ and Lord for all ages. Amen."

Day #29

Day #29
Rise, My King!

*"You seek the heights of manhood,
when you seek the depths of God."*

—*Edwin Luis Cole*

My Dear Brothers:

I am writing you this letter because I am still hearing of how many of you are trying to be players. Stories of how you haven't grasped the concept of being faithful and understanding manhood. How you feel that getting multiple women and money will somehow fill the hole that is gaping in your soul. It sounds like the media has dazzled you into a low-life destiny with the stench of Willie Lynch.

Lucy Larcom said, "The curse of covetousness is that it destroys manhood by substituting money for character." It is getting more difficult to defend you because there are so many books, seminars and speakers at your disposal for you to attend and to purchase for your freedom but you won't. Which is so sad when your freedom is but a few little choices away yet you refuse to grab it but rather hold on to your past pain because that is what you are used to.

It is depressing to me when I see you dressed and acting like women, stating that you were born this way or this is really who you are. Personally, I think you are confused.

There are women out there who are waiting for you to take your places as Kings so that they can take their places as Queens. When this happens, the family and community will be strengthened because of your example. Even better, for some of you, you will bless the nation.

I am coming to you now with urgency because the times are tumultuous and the last thing that I want for you is for you to come to the end of your life saying, "I should have; could have; would have . . ."

When a man comes into his destiny, it is powerful and beautiful. But it must start with him facing his giants and dealing with them. Sam Keen writes, "There are two questions a man must ask himself: 'Where am I going?' and 'Who will go with me?' These questions speak powerfully to purpose which makes a man so attractive. His focus must be purpose and not pleasure.

Larissa Lone said, "Let a woman too close and while she sucked your cock, she sucked your brains out of you, too." Normally I would not put such an explicit quote in my book but I want to make it painfully clear how important this is. There are manipulative women out there who will take you down.

The keys to your armor in manhood are discernment; focus; humility; mentorship and great, honest people. The world is about to open to you. Don't be afraid to put in your dues. Face your fears. Stay away from liars. Let the world hear your character sing. And may your enemies see you Rise.

Rise my King.

Rise!

Day #30

Day#30
Live On Purpose

.⌐■⌐.

"The purpose of life is a life of purpose."
– Robert Byrne

Life is so much better when it is lived on purpose. Intentionality is the soil for greatness. When you are being groomed to blossom and prepared by people who love you, there is no limit.

To go through life not knowing who you are, what you're learning style is or your love language, results in the inevitability of personal chaos. To quiet these storms within, you are just a few books away to put you on a course of joy, peace and true happiness.

Here are a few:

- 7 Habits of Highly Effective People
  – Stephen Covey

- The Five Languages of Love – Gary Chapman

- Rich Dad, Poor Dad – Robert Kyosiaki

- Instinct – Bishop T.D. Jakes

There are countless more, but these are a great start. I've heard several wealthy people say, "Readers are Leaders." For twenty years, I have been reading one self-help book a month and it has produced wonders. A couple of those books I have read at least twice because they have revolutionized my life. I love what Richelle E. Goodrich observed, "I'm starting to think that this world is just a place for us to learn that we need each other more than we want to admit."

Life is guaranteed to beat you up and take you through some unexpected drama. It wouldn't be life if it didn't. But, the ones who win are the ones who learn from their mistakes and learn on the shoulders of winners. The beautiful thing about where we are in life today is that we are in the Information Age. This is a time when information is plentiful and all at the tip of a finger, via cellphone and other small, electronic devices. We have so much access that it's scary. If we can choose wisely, we can do some incredible things with our lives, but it has to be on purpose.

This means discipline is going to have to be at the forefront of what we do. There is no greatness without discipline. This is very important to hear because the media is extremely disciplined in giving us a lot of toxicity to hear and to see.

Fifty percent of what we see and hear is how we learn. This means that we have to guard what we are seeing on a daily basis. Living on purpose means living with intention so that our souls can be pure. Amit Ray states, "Beauty is the purest feeling of the soul. Beauty arises when the soul is satisfied."

BONUS
Day #31

Day #31

Get A Massage!

"There are some things in life where it is better to receive than to give, and a massage is one of them."

– Al Michaels

I have had the fortunate pleasure of being a Massage Therapist for eight years. It is massively gratifying to see people come in stressed, in pain, and leave full of peace, pleasure and feeling elated. To bring such balance to one's day is a complete honor but, I agree with Al Michaels to receive a good massage is amazing. One of my clients said after her massage, "I feel like royalty," others have said things like, "You're the best" or "the best massage I've received in my life," while others were just pleasantly speechless. A massage is simply wonderful. I cannot stress enough the numerous health benefits that one receives by getting them regularly.

I would strongly recommend that you reassess your budget and find a way to place it in your monthly or bi-monthly routine. It will literally enhance your life. There have been times where I have been in pain, and struggled to move parts of my body, and after getting a massage, it not only relieved my physical pain but gave me new life. If you can't afford a spa try talking to a Licensed Massage Therapist and strike a deal for 30-45 minutes. Trust me, you need it and will not regret it.

Massage Therapy is a great stress reliever and I don't have to tell you that today we are in stressful times. On a personal note, I have massaged well over 6,000 people. 90% of them are white women; along with women of different races. I wish that had said 6,000 people with 3,000 women and 3,000 men. Too many men are caught up in the image of manhood and are not taking care of themselves. A massage will help them do that greatly. In addition, notice I said most of those women were white. One frustrating factor about blacks is we don't take care of ourselves and yet we are under tremendous stress.

Living like this is a death sentence slowly waiting to happen. A massage will literally lengthen your years. One author said, "I'd rather get a massage and get the problem rubbed out than taking a pill and feel drugged out."

The older I get, and I love getting older, I search for more healthy ways of living and more stressless ways of being prosperous, and having a massage is definitely included in the list of a more healthy way of living. I employ you to take this seriously. A lot of times the answers to our health and stress issues are right in front of our faces, but we are not paying attention. I've massaged thousands of people only once because they look at it as a birthday treat or a Valentines Day gift. When in actuality it is a beautiful way of life that will simply make you better on every level. This is something you want to pursue. I agree with the person who said, "Time spent getting a massage is never wasted." Get a massage! You'll be glad that you did.

Also by David Carruthers

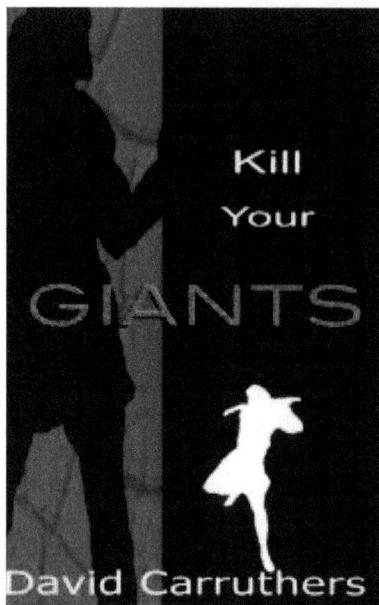

In his debut book **Kill Your Giants** Life Coach David Carruthers offers practical and powerful tools to overcome fear and rejection, deal with anger, manage lust, and conquer the dangers of pride.

This book will transform your thinking and catapult you towards your emotional and financial destiny.

"A very inspirational book; It has helped me in my dedication to my career. I will recommend it to my friends."

— Carlos Castillo

Kill Your Giants Personal Development Program is a 7 week upbeat, interactive course where students learn how to overcome issues that impede their progress and get practical tools that produces, purpose, confidence and character.

"This workshop that you did was amazing. It got us thinking

and it really helps us with our life.

— Arie

"I will never forget this class because it helped me realize that my dreams are closer then they seem."

— Sierra

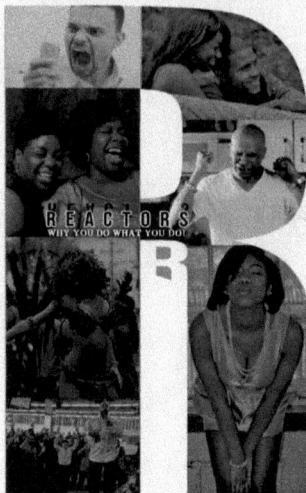

"This book defines the process that many need to cope with the constant pressure of today's Media-Driven World." — Bryant Cyr.

DAVID CARRUTHERS

REACTORS

WHY YOU DO WHAT YOU DO!

"The longer I live, the more confident I am that we all have more leadership potential that we think we have. David Carruthers' book, believed, then implemented with prayerful courage, will prompt us further in that direction. We will thank him for it, and God will say to us, "Well done, good and faithful servant."

— Rev. Raph Kee, Author, Professor, Gordon Conwell

Once again David has pushed the envelope of discussion. Mr. Carruthers is masterful at invoking conversation about topics that make us uncomfortable. Great job!

— Steve Galloway, Author The Deconstruction of the American Culture

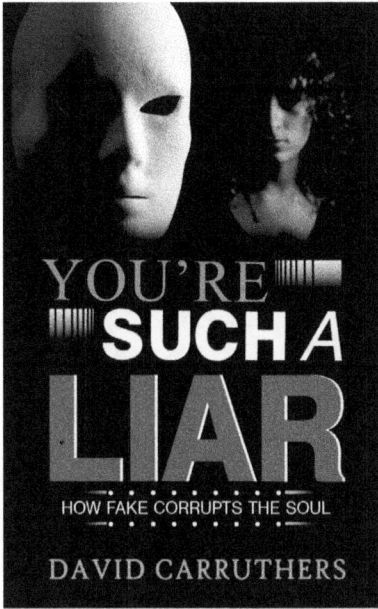

"You're Such A Liar" is an inspirational account of the way in which many people struggle with finding their real purpose and destiny through self-discovery of authenticity. Through the author's personal life experiences and testimony, readers will be able to view a firsthand account of the way in which people can deter you from stepping into the great person God has called you to be. The motivational quotes in You're Such A Liar serve as a reflection tool for people to examine their past failures and plan for a successful future. The author makes notes of various Biblical examples to reinforce the notion that all truths and answers rely in God.

Through the use of motivational quotes, poetry, as well as Bible verses, the author allows readers to re-visit past situations and while offering Godly solutions to real life issues. The Author addresses serious social issues plaguing our society that many people fail or refuse to address resulting from their own fear. The author confronts complex issues regarding gender roles and identity while providing tools to prevent broken families. God is authentic and real in every way. In order to step into your purpose and destiny, it is important that you confront yourself, and remove the barriers because we all know, Fake Doesn't Last.

— Pastor Monterial Bynoe
The TOP Church,
Randolph MA